ENDANGERED
FOREST ANIMALS

Dave Taylor

Crabtree Publishing Company

Toronto·Oxford·New York

ENDANGERED ANIMALS SERIES

Text and photographs by Dave Taylor

For Stephen

Editor-in-chief
Bobbie Kalman

Editors
Janine Schaub
Shelagh Wallace

Design and computer layout
Antoinette "Cookie" DeBiasi

Cover mechanicals
Diane Coderre

Type output
Lincoln Graphics

Color separations
ISCOA

Printer
Worzalla Publishing

Published by
Crabtree Publishing Company

350 Fifth Avenue	6900 Kinsmen Court	73 Lime Walk
Suite 3308	P.O. Box 1000	Headington
New York	Niagara Falls, ON	Oxford OX3 7AD
N.Y. 10118	Canada L2E 7E7	United Kingdom

940047

Cataloguing in Publication Data
Taylor, Dave, 1948-
　Endangered forest animals

(The Endangered animals series)
Includes index.
ISBN 0-86505-529-7 (library bound) ISBN 0-86505-539-4 (pbk.)

1. Forest fauna - Juvenile literature.
2. Endangered species - Juvenile literature.
3. Wildlife conservation - Juvenile literature.
I. Title. II. Series: Taylor, Dave, 1948-
The endangered animals series.

QL112.T38 1992　　j591.52'909152

Contents

The world's forests

Some forests are humid jungles; others are cool, wet places with giant, towering trees. There are forests filled with maples, birches, oaks, and aspen that turn beautiful colors in the autumn. Although forests may look quite different, they all have one thing in common—trees are their most plentiful plant.

Evergreen forests

Trees with cones and waxy needles are called **evergreens**. They keep their green needles all year. Evergreen forests can survive in cold, harsh climates. In the northern part of Europe, Asia, and North America, evergreen forests are known as **taiga**.

Deciduous forests

Deciduous trees lose all their leaves when the weather turns cold. The leaves of many deciduous trees turn spectacular shades of red, orange, and yellow before they drop to the ground. Deciduous forests are found where the climate is moderate and wet. They cover the eastern part of the United States, most of Europe, and small parts of eastern Asia.

Mixed forests

Deciduous trees are often part of mixed forests that include evergreens. Scientists call mixed forests **transition zones**, or change areas, because one type of forest blends into another. Mixed forests are located between the taiga and the deciduous forests.

The rainforest

Rainforests are located in areas where there is a lot of rain. There are two types of rainforests: the **temperate rainforest** and the **tropical rainforest**. The temperate rainforest is found in cool, wet climates along the West Coast of North America. Very little of this forest is left. The temperate rainforest produces tall, giant trees. Most of these trees have been cut down by the logging industry.

The tropical rainforest is found in central Africa, Southeast Asia, along the Amazon River in South America, and in northern Australia and the surrounding islands. It, too, is being logged both for its timber and for the cleared land, which is then used for planting crops.

Supporting animal life

The warmer and wetter a forest is, the more types of plants it supports. The northern taiga has only a few types of trees, whereas the tropical rainforest has hundreds of types of trees. Because animals eat different parts of various trees, the northern forests have fewer types of plants from which animals can choose. The richest type of forest in terms of animal life is the tropical rainforest. A single tree may have thousands of creatures living on it.

Forests are found all over the world. The one in the picture on the opposite page is a rainforest in Africa. Rainforests support thousands of species of animals.

Animals in distress

In recent years, people have forced many kinds of animals to struggle for survival. Hunting, farming, and the loss of wilderness areas have made life difficult and sometimes impossible for thousands of species of animals.

Worldwide conservation groups have developed various terms to describe animals in distress. Animals that are **extinct** have not been seen in the wild for over fifty years. Animals referred to as **endangered** are likely to die out if their situation is not improved. **Threatened** animals are endangered in some areas where they live. **Rare** animals are species with small populations that may be at risk.

There is a concern for all animals living in the wild. Even if some species are not yet threatened or endangered, they may lose their lives because of pollution or loss of their homes. There is hope, however. Due to the efforts of conservation groups, many animals that once faced extinction are now surviving in healthy numbers again.

*Many of the forest animals in this book are endangered because they have been hunted or trapped. The biggest danger to forests and the creatures that make forests their home, however, is **habitat** destruction. Many of the world's forests have already been cut down for lumber or cleared to make way for farms, mines, dams, and cities. Without the forest for a home, cougars, parrots, and elephants alike will not survive.*

The tapir, above, is found in the rainforests surrounding the Amazon River in South America. Young tapirs have striped and spotted coats to camouflage them from predators, especially jaguars. If this tapir could talk, what do you think he would be saying?

The gibbon's powerful arms allow it to swing through the trees with ease. All nine species of gibbons are now endangered as their forest homes are being harvested for lumber.

Chimpanzees eat a variety of foods. They like bananas and other fruits that grow in the forests, but they also eat insects, seeds, and sometimes even hunt and kill other animals for food.

Chimpanzees are one of the few types of animals that make their own tools. They have been observed stripping leaves off twigs and using the twigs to pull termites out of a den for a tasty snack.

The chimpanzee

Chimpanzees are very intelligent animals. They remind people of human beings. Chimps have many facial expressions that are similar to those of people. Because their bodies are somewhat like ours, chimps also have human-like movements.

Medical research

Chimpanzees are a kind of ape; they are our closest living relative in the animal world. Chimps have similar body organs to those of human beings and can suffer from the same diseases. For this reason, they are often used to test new machines or surgical techniques before these are used on people.

Chummy chimps

In the wild, chimps live in groups of up to forty animals. These groups consist of several females and their children. Mothers and daughters remain close throughout their lives. Sons and brothers also have family ties. They protect their relatives against chimpanzee bullies.

Saving the chimp

In the past, thousands of chimpanzees were removed from their wilderness homes. They were used in laboratories, sold to the entertainment industry, and kept as pets. Today many more chimps are dying because their habitats are being destroyed by loggers and farmers. Because these animals are now endangered, new laws have been passed to protect them. National parks offer the best hope of saving wild chimps from extinction.

Height: 24-48 inches (61-122 centimeters)
Weight: 55-110 pounds (25-50 kilograms)
Where it lives: The rainforest, open woodlands, and grasslands of western and central Africa

Chimpanzees have loud voices and make many noises including roars, screams, and grunts. Sometimes they drum on tree trunks.

The Siberian tiger

The Siberian tiger is not only the largest tiger on earth, it is also the largest of all the world's cats. Most people think of tigers as living in warm, moist jungles, but the Siberian tiger is found in places where there is deep snow—in the mountain forests of Russia and China in a region known as Siberia.

cattle if food is scarce. Sometimes the tiger eats the villagers, too. That is why this beautiful cat has been hunted almost to extinction. People do not like big animals that threaten to eat them!

Life at the zoo

Scientists think that there are fewer than 200 Siberian tigers left in the wild, but there are many times that number in zoos and circuses. These big cats breed well in captivity, and zoos often have to control the number of cubs that are born there. If there are so many Siberian tigers living in zoos, why is there a concern that these cats might become extinct?

Scientists point out that a zoo-bred tiger is not the same as a wild one. Captive tigers do not have to hunt for their food. They are cared for and do not face the dangers of the wild.

Return to the wild?

Could the captive Siberian tigers survive if they were returned to their native habitats? The truth is that no one really knows for certain. Conservation groups hope to save enough wild cats so that zoo animals will not have to be released for scientific studies. In the meantime, so little is known about wild Siberian tigers that the task at hand is to learn more about their natural ways.

The large bodies of Siberian tigers produce more heat to keep them warm in their cold habitats.

Big appetites

Like all cats, Siberian tigers eat meat. They prey upon the mountain sheep and elk and will hunt villagers' sheep and

Length: (with tail) 9 feet (3 meters)
Weight: Up to 850 pounds (385 kilograms)
Where it lives: As far north as the Arctic Circle in Asia

The gray wolf

In some parts of their range, wolves are very common. Canada, Alaska, and Russia still have large numbers of wolves. In other parts of their traditional habitats, however, especially in the United States, Europe, and Mexico, there may be only a few hundred animals left.

The killing of wolves

Wolves have had a bad reputation for a long time. In Europe and Asia, there are countless stories of wolves attacking people. For this reason, people felt they had to kill as many wolves as possible. Another reason people killed wolves is that wolves were believed to prey mainly on animals that supplied people with meat. Hunters did not like to lose deer to wolves, and farmers did not want their sheep and cattle eaten. As people began living in places where wolves roamed, the wolves were trapped and shot until only a few were left.

Wolves do not deserve the bad reputation people have given them through stories and books. Most wolves are social animals that live in small packs and care for one another. They generally keep away from people and populated areas.

The wolf howls that many people find frightening are the animal's way of communicating with other wolves. It is a way of marking the location of a pack's territory and a warning for other wolves to stay away. Wolves may also howl because they enjoy it.

Important predators

Scientists who study wolves have discovered that they mostly hunt small animals such as mice. When wolves hunt larger animals, they seek out the sick and weak members of the herd.

Plans for reintroduction

In places where all the wolves were killed, deer herds have grown so large that after a bad winter thousands of deer die of starvation. The solution to this problem would be to reintroduce wolves into areas where they once lived. The wolves would keep the deer population healthy and under control. Unfortunately, farmers, hunters, and ranchers do not want wolves back again and are fighting to stop this plan. It may be some time before wolves are removed from the endangered species list and are returned safely all over their range.

Height: 26-38 inches (66-97 centimeters)
Length: 50-70 inches (127-178 centimeters)
Weight: 60-157 pounds (27-71 kilograms)
Where it lives: The northern half of North America, parts of Europe, and all of Asia except India and the jungle regions of China

The jaguar

Jaguars used to live in deserts and jungles. Today most are found in jungles; those living in open areas are more easily killed. As more and more of the rainforest is being cut down, jaguars have less wilderness area in which to live and hunt. Another reason that the jaguar population is so low is that these cats were hunted in the past for their beautiful fur.

A varied diet

Unlike many cats, the jaguar loves water and will sometimes hunt the crocodiles and snakes that live in the jungle swamps. It also eats monkeys, deer, sloths, tapirs, turtles, eggs, frogs, fish, and anything else it can catch.

Roar or purr?

The jaguar is the largest cat in North and South America. It is a member of the big-cat family and is related to the lion, tiger, and leopard. Scientists group cats by their voice boxes. All the members of the big-cat family can roar, whereas the other cats cannot. A jaguar's roar sounds like a loud cough; the house cat, the lynx, and the mountain lion purr instead of roaring.

Home on the range

Jaguars have home ranges called territories. These areas are usually quite large—up to two hundred square miles (518 square kilometers). Jaguars need these large territories because they often have to travel long distances to find food. Sometimes the territory of two jaguars overlaps, but the cats usually avoid each other. The only time a jaguar seeks out another jaguar is at mating time.

Jaguar cubs

Once a female has bred, she goes off on her own and gives birth to between one and four babies. The cubs are blind and helpless when they are born, but they begin seeing clearly in about two weeks. The cubs stay with their mother for almost a year before leaving to establish their own territories. Jaguars are fully grown by the age of three.

The future of jaguars depends on the market for their fur coats and the size of the jungle territory that people are willing to leave for them and other wild dwellers.

Height: 27-30 inches (69-76 centimeters)
Length: (with tail) 70-100 inches (178-254 centimeters)
Weight: 120-300 pounds (54-136 kilograms)
Where it lives: Southwestern United States, Mexico, and South America

---

Most jaguars are gold with black markings, but there are also jaguars with black fur.

Jaguars are often confused with leopards, but there are many differences. Jaguars are found in South America, whereas leopards live in Africa and Asia. Leopards are smaller and have narrow heads and bodies. Their markings are clumps of black spots; a jaguar's are more like rings with dots in the center.

The lowland gorilla

Gorillas are animals found in the lowlands and mountains of Africa. The lowland gorilla is more common than the mountain gorilla, although both types are threatened by the activities of people. Fewer than 1,000 mountain gorillas and only a few thousand lowland gorillas are left in the wild. Gorillas are threatened by poachers who take their heads as trophies and by people who are destroying their forest homes.

The gorilla band
Gorillas live in small bands or groups with one large male, several females, and their young. Groups of more than ten gorillas are rare. The bands stay together for long periods of time and live in the same general area. They move too slowly to travel very far and spend much of their day eating and digesting their food.

At home on the ground
Old Tarzan movies often show gorillas swinging through trees but, in fact, gorillas live most of their lives on the ground. They climb trees only when threatened or when there is some really tasty food at the top.

When gorillas go to sleep, they build nests by bending branches and grasses and shaping them into cuplike beds. These beds may be on the ground or in a

Gorilla babies like playing and wrestling. The mother in the left picture is given a surprise pinch by her mischievous baby. She distracts him with a piggyback ride.

tree. The larger the gorilla, the more likely that the nest will be on the ground. Lowland gorillas keep very clean nests that are made fresh every night.

Life in captivity

Lowland gorillas are the apes most often seen in zoos. They were brought to the zoos as young animals, after their parents were killed during their capture. It was once thought that for every baby gorilla that was shipped to a zoo, at least two adults were killed. Today, no zoo buys babies taken this way. Zoos get their new gorillas from those born in captivity. These zoo-bred gorillas do not know much about life in the wild.

Playful baby apes

Gorilla babies are much like human babies. They enjoy playing with their mothers and with each other and love to wrestle. Their mothers teach them how to find food, and they spend a big part of their day eating leaves, bark, and fruit. Young female gorillas stay with their mother's group, but young males leave to join another group when they are a few years old.

Height: Female: 4.5-5 feet (1.4-1.5 meters)
Male: 5.5-6 feet (1.7-1.8 meters)
Weight: Female: 200 pounds (90 kilograms)
Male: 310-400 pounds (140-180 kilograms)
Where it lives: The coastal nations of West Africa that border the equator

Mandrills (above) are very colorful animals, whereas drills (below) have dark fur and shiny black faces.

The mandrill and drill

The mandrill and its close relative the drill are forest-living baboons. They are incredibly strong and heavy-set animals that can live for as long as forty years. Both types of baboons have striking appearances and can look quite fearsome when they flash their fanged teeth during a loud bark.

Mandrills and drills are threatened by the destruction of their forest homes. In the past, the mandrill's meat was considered a delicacy in West African markets. Although the drill is the most endangered, both baboons are protected today.

More colorful than a rainbow

The mandrill is the most brightly colored mammal in the world. Sky blue, scarlet red, flaming orange, jet black, snow white, and bright pink are all colors found on this animal. The male mandrill has especially colorful skin on its face and bottom. Scientists do not agree on the importance of the mandrill's coloring. Some believe male mandrills use their colors to frighten other animals; others say that the colors may be used to attract females or even help mandrills identify one another.

The drill

The drill is slightly smaller than the mandrill and lacks the colorful markings. Drill fur is mainly a dark olive color, and the animal's face is shiny black. Like the mandrill, the drill has a brightly colored area on its body—its hairless bottom that can be bright pink, red, or blue. On both buttocks there is a tough area of skin called a **callus**.

Traveling troops

Both mandrills and drills live in small groups called **troops**. They spend most of their time on the ground searching for food, but move to the trees to eat and sleep. They feed on a variety of foods ranging from seeds and insects to small animals. In order to protect their young, these baboons throw sticks and stones at possible enemies.

Height: Mandrill (with tail) 24-41 inches (62-105 centimeters) Drill (with tail) 20-40 inches (51-102 centimeters)
Weight: 110 pounds (50 kilograms)
Where they live: Central Africa

The orangutan

Chimps, gorillas, and orangutans are all large apes. The first two spend a lot of their time on the ground. The orangutan is the one that is most at home in the forest. Its long powerful arms and handlike feet are perfect for swinging from branches and moving from tree to tree. It is rare for an adult orangutan ever to touch the forest floor, and when it does, it has an awkward way of walking.

Feast in the trees

Orangutans like fruit best of all, but they will eat leaves, nuts, and shoots. They also eat insects, young birds, and squirrels when they can catch them. They drink water that collects in tree holes by sticking their arms into the water and then catching the droplets in their mouths.

Mother orangutans take good care of their babies.

Solitary swingers

Orangutans spend most of their lives alone. Females with young are the exception; they have their first babies when they are about ten or eleven years old. The baby is nursed by its mother for about three years before it is weaned and ready to share its mother's diet.

A long childhood

The baby stays with its mother for up to four years before it goes off on its own. This long childhood means that the mother can teach the baby the things it needs to know in order to survive. There may be four years between the birth of one baby and the next.

Young orangutans sometimes find other orangutans their age to play with before going back to spend the night with their mothers. Adult orangutans never play.

Fighting for space

Male orangutans have a territory that overlaps that of several females. When other males come into the territory that is already occupied, a hooting match begins. The territorial male tries to scare the other males away, but if that does not work, a fight takes place. Most adult males over fifteen years old carry scars from such battles.

Orangutan battles are more common today. As the rainforests are being cut down, the orangutans are forced into smaller and smaller territories, where fighting is more likely to occur.

Height: Female: 52 inches (132 centimeters) Male: 54 inches (137 centimeters)
Weight: Female: 88-110 pounds (40-50 kilograms) Male: 130-200 pounds (60-90 kilograms)
Where it lives: Northern Sumatra and Borneo in Southeast Asia

The name "orangutan" means "man of the forest." When you look at the face of one, it is easy to see why native people thought these animals were men.

The Asian elephant

Today there are fewer than 50,000 wild Asian elephants left in the world. That number is decreasing quickly for several reasons. The Asian elephant's natural home is the tropical forests of India and Asia. Much of this habitat has now been destroyed. As farmers clear more of the forest to plant crops, many elephants must move to the open plains, where they are easy targets for hunters and traders. Most wild elephants are now found in a few national parks.

Hard-working animals

For hundreds of years, people have been using Asian elephants to lift logs, pull heavy loads, and carry people. Almost all these elephants have come from the wild and were tamed. Very few were born in captivity. Being a beast of burden for centuries has caused the Asian elephant to become an endangered species.

No time for babies

The people who use elephants for labor do not want their elephants to have babies because that means the mother elephant cannot work for several years while she is looking after her youngster. Instead of allowing the animals to have babies, the elephant owners catch new wild elephants to replace the aging ones. This means that the wild herds keep getting smaller.

Astounding appetites

An Asian elephant feeds sixteen hours a day. It eats 400 pounds (181 kilograms) of leaves, shoots, branches, and grasses during that time. Elephants must always be near water because they drink about 61 gallons (230 liters) daily! They produce huge mounds of manure that contain many nutrients on which birds and other creatures feed.

Big differences

Asian elephants are also known as Indian elephants. Their closest living relative is the African elephant, but the two are actually quite different. African elephants have larger ears (the shape of Africa, some say), a straighter back, larger tusks, wrinkled skin, and a trunk that has two fingers at its tip. An Asian elephant has small ears (the shape of India, others say), a rounded back, smaller tusks, smoother skin, and only one finger on its trunk.

Height: 8-9 feet (2.5-3 meters)
Length: 18-21 feet (5.5-6.4 meters)
Weight: 11,000 pounds (5000 kilograms)
Where it lives: India and Southeast Asia

When it is born, an Asian elephant weighs about 200 pounds (90 kilograms). If it is a female, it will stay with its mother's herd all its life. If it is a male, it will leave the herd and join a small group of other males when it is eleven or twelve.

Parrots

Most people have only seen parrots in bird cages, but parrots live in flocks in the tropical rainforests. They are colorful, intelligent birds that can live up to 80 years. There are 315 species of parrots, ranging in size from as small as a sparrow to about 3 feet (almost a meter) in length.

Clever beak and toes

All parrots have large heads, thick, sharply hooked beaks, short necks, and **prehensile** feet. Prehensile feet have toes that allow an animal to grip branches or hang upside-down. Their beaks act as a kind of third foot, which parrots use for lifting themselves onto branches.

Taste testers

Parrots fly from tree to tree, feeding on the many fruits, nuts, and seeds in the forest. They are well known for their choosy palates. Parrots sample every-thing with their fleshy, dark tongues before they eat it.

Nesting cooperation

Most parrots nest in tree hollows, although some find spots in burrows on the ground or in rock cracks or caves. While the female is sitting on her eggs, she does not leave the nest. Her mate tirelessly brings food to her during this time. When the chicks hatch, they are cared for by both parents. The parents collect food and soften it in their **crops** before feeding it to their young.

Shrieks and squawks

Parrots have a reputation for being noisy birds and excellent imitators. One species of parrot, the African gray, can mimic almost any sound from "Polly want a cracker?" to the noise of a washing machine. All parrots make sounds deep in their throats. They "talk" with their beaks closed and look like ventriloquists.

From the wild to the pet shop

In order to meet the world demand for pet-shop parrots, thousands of these birds are captured each year. For this reason, several species of parrots are threatened with extinction in the wild. Hundreds are killed in an effort to catch a few live ones, and many more die on their journeys to pet shops.

Picking parrots as pets

If you are thinking of owning a parrot, you should insist that yours is one that has been hatched in captivity. Many pet stores today only sell parrots from captive breeders because the owners know that the population of wild parrots will continue to decrease unless all illegal trade of parrots is stopped!

Height: 4-40 inches (10-102 centimeters)
Where they live: Tropical rainforests of Central America, South America, Australia, and Africa.

Parrots are known by other names such as cockatoo, conure, cockatiel, and kakapo.

There are more than three hundred species of parrots. Most, such as the ones on this page, have colorful feathers. Many people want parrots as pets because they are colorful and because some of them are able to talk. This popularity has endangered the existence of parrots in the wild.

The eastern cougar

When North American pioneers began the business of clearing the land, they also killed all the cougars that they sighted in the forests. Later, farmers and ranchers shot more cougars because they believed cougars were dangerous to people and livestock. By the 1860s scientists thought that one member of this cat family, the eastern cougar, was extinct.

Protection too late?

In the 1940s a few sightings were reported. People claimed to have seen the eastern cougar and its tracks in Canadian forests. The eastern cougar was given full protection as an endangered species, but was this move too late? No one could be certain that this big cat was alive because so few were sighted.

Cougar confusion

Fewer than a dozen skulls and skins of the eastern cougar exist in museums. These remains are not enough to judge for certain what makes eastern cougars different from other cougars. Many people wonder whether the eastern cougars that have been seen recently are really western cougars. All cougars have similar light brown to gray coloring, small heads, and long tails, making it difficult to tell the species apart.

Cautious cat

The eastern cougar, like all cougars, is a secretive animal. Although cougars are the second-largest member of the cat family in North America (only the jaguar is bigger), few people have ever seen one. Cougars live alone except when breeding or when the female has her cubs.

A question of time

In the United States, the eastern cougar lives in habitats ranging from mangrove swamps to hardwood forests. It can live in both desert and snow, but it needs some wooded areas for shelter and an abundant supply of prey such as deer, porcupine, beaver, muskrat, and raccoon. The eastern cougar may be extinct in Canada. It is up to people to make sure it does not suffer the same fate elsewhere.

Length: 65-100 inches (165-254 centimeters)
Weight: 80-225 pounds (36-102 kilograms)
Where it lives: Eastern North America

The cougar is known by several other names: puma, mountain lion, and panther. Next to the jaguar, it is the largest North American cat. Cougars can be brown, yellow, or even gray. Their fur is soft and short, but cougars that live in northern regions have longer fur.

Saving the world's forests

Forests are very important to the animals mentioned in this book; they provide them with food, water, and shelter. Forests are important to people, too. Lumber, paper products, rubber, and even some types of medicines come from the trees found in forests. Forests help keep our air moist and fresh, and forest parklands are beautiful places for visiting or camping.

Killing the forests

In many areas of the world, logging companies are not required by their governments to plant new trees to replace the ones that have been cut down. Logging companies often **clearcut** whole areas. Clearcutting means that every last tree is cut down and only some are taken away to be used. This procedure severely damages the environment and causes millions of creatures to lose their homes. Some kinds of plants and animals die and disappear from the earth forever.

A beef about beef

Raising beef cattle can be a major threat to the survival of forests. Many fast-food outlets sell hamburgers that are made out of beef that comes from ranches located where rainforests once stood. Don't buy food in restaurants that get their meat from regions that were once forests. At least one big fast-food chain makes a point of stating that it never buys from these places. Find out which restaurants do not buy rainforest beef and give them your support and business.

Writing letters

Some forests are being needlessly destroyed. Write to your local government representative to find out what is happening to the forests in your area and ask questions such as these:
• Are forests being logged in the area? What harvesting methods are being used?
• If clearcutting is taking place, can it be discontinued and replaced with a less destructive type of logging?
• Are new trees being planted?
• Are dams being constructed that will flood huge forest areas? Are these dams necessary, or are there alternatives?

Planting new trees

Many people around the world are shocked that so many forests are being cut down each year. It takes forests many years to grow back, but trees do grow. Thousands of conservation-minded people are now taking part in planting new trees in parks, school grounds, and in their own back yards. Get involved in planting trees! It will make you feel good, and your tree will provide animals with food and shelter.

Buy a piece of a rainforest

You and your friends can pool your finances and buy an acre of rainforest. By buying part of a rainforest, you will save that area from being cut down. Your local environment groups can give you details on how to make your purchase. Get your school involved and buy several acres!

One easy way to save trees is by practicing the three Rs: reducing, reusing, and recycling. You can help reduce the number of trees that are being cut down by reusing paper, trading or giving away your magazines, and by taking part in newspaper and fine-paper recycling programs. Every bit helps!

Every living creature, including human beings, needs forests. Forests give us clean air, and they keep soil from being washed away. They keep the areas around them moist and cool. Forests provide homes for thousands of species of animals. Saving forests is everybody's business. Make it yours!

Glossary

burrow A hole dug in the ground by an animal in which it lives and hides

callus A hard and thick area of skin

clearcutting A method of cutting trees whereby all trees in an area are cut down and only some are used

conservation Protection from loss, harm, or waste, especially of natural resources, such as wildlife

crop A pouch in which food is prepared for digestion

deciduous A kind of plant that sheds its leaves each year

endangered Threatened with extinction

evergreen A kind of plant that has green leaves or needles throughout the year

extinct Not in existence; not seen in the wild for over fifty years

flock A gathering of one kind of animal

habitat The natural environment of a plant or animal

hardwood Describing broad-leaved, flowering trees

harvest To gather a crop when it is ripe

livestock Domestic animals, such as pigs, cows, and sheep

lowland Land on a lower level than the surrounding land

lumber The planks and boards that have been cut from trees

mangrove Tropical evergreen trees found in marshy areas

national park An area of land maintained for public use by the government

poacher A person who hunts illegally

predator An animal that captures and eats other animals

prehensile Adapted for grasping something

prey An animal hunted by another animal for food

rainforest A dense forest in an area of high annual rainfall

range An area over which animals roam and find food

rare Uncommon; in serious danger of becoming extinct

recycle To make waste material suitable for reuse by treating or processing it in some way

reduce To make smaller; to bring under control

reintroduction The bringing in of wild animals to regions where they once lived

reputation The way in which people think of a person or thing

reuse To use again

Siberia A large northern area of the Soviet Union

species A group of related plants or animals that can produce young together

taiga Evergreen forests of northernmost Europe, Asia, and North America

temperate Describing a climate that has no extreme highs or lows in temperature

territory Any area that an animal considers its own

threatened Endangered in some parts of its habitat

troop A group or flock

tropical Hot and humid; describing an area close to the equator

wean To make a young animal used to food other than its mother's milk

Index

3 4 5 6 7 8 9 0 Printed in USA 1 0 9 8 7 6 5 4 3